WORD WOUNDS

AND

WATER FLOWERS

POEMS

BY

DANIELA GIOSEFFI

BORDIGHERA INCORPORATED
WEST LAFAYETTE, IN

© 1995 by Daniela Gioseffi.

All rights reserved. Poems may be reprinted only by written permission from the author, and may not be reproduced for publication in book, magazine, or electronic media of any kind, except in quotations for purposes of literary reviews by critics.

Printed in the United States.

Published by
Bordighera, Inc.
Purdue University
1359 Stanley Coulter Hall
West Lafayette, IN 47907-1359

VIA FOLIOS 4
ISBN 1-884419-03-8

ACKNOWLEDGEMENTS

Grateful acknowledgement is made to the editors of the following periodicals and anthologies in which some of these poems first appeared:

MAGAZINES:
Ambit (England), *Antaeus, Choice, Confrontation, Contact II, The Nation, Nine Apples, The Manhattan Poetry Review, Oxford Magazine, The Paris Review, New Moon; Tamarack: The Journal of the Millay Society, The Review of the Poetry Society of America; The Croton Review; The Kentucky Review, Redstart, Nomad, Poetry East, VIA: Voices in Italian Americana, Italian Americana, The Long Islander, The Manhattan Poetry Review, The Journal of New Jersey Poets, Footwork, The Paterson Literary Review.* "Blood Autumn" was 1990 winner of the "Eve of St. Agnes National Poetry Award," judged by Leo Conellan and awarded by Sue Walker, editor, *Negative Capability*, at The University of Alabama, Mobile.

ANTHOLOGIES:
"Wheat" appeared in *Contemporaries*, ed. Jean Malley and Hale Tokay, Viking Press, New York, 1972; and in *Structure and Meaning; An Introduction to Literature*, ed. Anthony Dube, Houghton Mifflin, Boston, 1983; "After Drinking Water," in *We Become New: Poems of Contemporary American Women*, ed. Lucille Iverson and Kathyrn Ruby, Bantam Books, New York, 1975; "The Blind Soprano," *From A to Z; Contemporary American Poets*, ed. by David Ray, Swallow Press and Ohio University Press, Chicago and London, 1981; Prologue to "Through the I of the Needle," *The Ardis Anthology of New American Poetry*, ed. David Rigsbee and Ellendea Proffer, The Ardis Press, Ann Arbor, Michigan, 1977; "Through the I of the Needle," in *Poems of Death and Suicide*, ed. Lloyd L. Mills, Shelly's Chapbook Series, Ravenna, Ohio University, 1978; "Some Slippery Afternoon," *Literature; Options for Reading and Writing*, ed. D. Daiker, Harper & Row, New York, 1985; "Sonnets for my Father," *The Dream Book*, ed. Helen Barolini, Schocken Books, New York, 1985. "Toward the Greater Romance, Please Place

Roses in My Skull," *Deep Down*, ed. Laura Chester, Faber & Faber, London, 1988; Sections of: "The Exotic Enemy" and "Word Wounds, Water Flowers," *Women on War*, Touchstone, Simon & Schuster, New York 1988; "As When Some Silenced Singer Hears Her Aria, Aperture," from *From the Margin; Writings in Italian Americana*, ed. Anthony Julian Tamburri, Paolo Giordano, and Fred Gardaphe, Purdue University Press, 1991, 1994. "Unfinished Autobiography" appeared in *On Prejudice: A Global Perpective*, Anchor, Doubleday, New York, 1993. "American Sonnets to My Father," and "Grandma Lucia La Rosa" a.k.a. "Bicentennial Antipoem for Italian-American Women," appeared in *Unsettling America*, ed. Maria Mazziotti Gillan and Jennifer Gillan, Viking Penguin Press, New York, 1994.

A MEMORIAL DEDICATION

Because he gave me his immigrant tenacity to seek justice and live for poetry, this book is dedicated to *la memoria di mio padre*, **Donato Gioseffi**, *nato nel 1906, Orta Nova, Provincia di Puglia, Italia*, who died, 1981, in America. He ventured through Isola delle lacrime, "The Island of Tears" [Ellis Island] in 1913, with his mother Lucia La Rosa of Naples, surviving a miserable, but hopefilled, journey across the Atlantic on The USS Independence. Though disabled, sickly and poor, he shined shoes and sold newspapers to work his way through degrees from Union College and Columbia University. He was among the first Italian immigrants to achieve honors, a Phi Beta Kappa and Sigma Psi, in the Liberal Arts and Sciences from such societies. Though he spoke no English upon his arrival in the U.S., and was taunted as a "guinea gimp" by his American schoolmates, he was proud of his U.S. Citizenship, achieved in his twenties, and read to me through my youth from Dante, Rabelais, Cervantes and Shakespeare in perfect English, though he also spoke Italian fluently, making me proud of his first homeland. His final words were quoted from Prospero's in "The Tempest": *"The rarer action is in virtue than in vengeance,"* giving me an aesthetic ideal for action as his ultimate philosophy. This paragraph is offered as a tribute to all who share the memory of their immigrant or enslaved parents' struggle in America.

These poems are dedicated to my artist daughter, Thea Rinaldi Kearney, and my husband, Lionel B. Luttinger, with thanks for their supportiveness. And, it is dedicated to my five step children, especially Nina, and to all young people everywhere who keep a *planetary conscience* blooming in the light—as non-violent activists like Grace Paley, Maya Angelou, Helen Caldicott, Judy Bari, Petra Kelly, Eleanor Roosevelt, Jane Addams, Emily Green Balch, W.E.B. DuBois, Lucretia Mott, Martin Luther King Jr., Rosa Parks, Nelson Mandela, Linus Pauling,

Leo Tolstoy, Mahatma Gandhi, Chi'u Chin, Vittoria Colonna, Enhueduanna, and so many other *true* heroes and heroines of the worldwide, green peace movement inspire us and show us the way through the night to a new day in which, even so, "we shall overcome." *Cynical sorrow gives no light to action and sheds no beauty in its wake,* my father would say. *But, sorrow wedded deeply to a love as beauty, makes human miracles happen everyday.*

TABLE OF CONTENTS

PART I: BLOOD AUTUMN

Unfinished Autobiography	3
For Grandma Lucia La Rosa, *"Light the Rose,"*	7
American Sonnets for My Father, *for Donato Gioseffi* [*b. Italia: 1906—d. America: 1981*]	9
Guilt Is a Gift That Is Given	11
The Girl with Purple Hair	12
The Practical Nurse	14
The Thumbless Bus Driver	15
The Mother at the Zoo	17
The Blind Soprano Sings, *for Cheryl Taylor*	18
Jazz Lady of the Subway	19
Aeschylus Chorus	20
On Top of the Empire State	22
Cento at Dawn	26
Blood Autumn	27

PART II: ANIMAL INTIMACIES

After Our Argument, We Canoe	33
Returning from Paradise We Stop at a Carnival	35
Sheepdog of the City	36
Toward the Greater Romance, Please Place Roses in My Skull	37
The Ruby Throated Hummingbirds Are Gone	38
Winter Dark	39
Beneath the Dreaming Tree	41
The Language of Light, *for my dying "Wandering Angus"*	42
Sunlight	44
April Loon	45
The Pregnant Gardener	47
The Guillotine and the Cathedral, *for Alejo Carpentier*	48
The Sign of the Cross, *for Gertrude Stein*	49
Oh, Anus, Through the Centuries, *for Yang Chu, Taoist Philosopher*	50
The Olive Branch	51

PART III: WORD WOUNDS AND WATER FLOWERS

Word Wounds and Water Flowers	55
I. Where can mad money be spent	55
II. Walt Whitman's voice extolled these states and stars	55
III. Have you noticed how angry women are now	56
IV. There's no exotic enemy!	57
V. These are the word wounds	58
VI. There are those mornings	59
VII. There are still those days when peace reigns	60
VIII. In civilized rooms	60
IX. We are all one human creature bound by earth	62

PART IV: THROUGH THE "I" OF THE NEEDLE

Wheat	65
Matrimonial Bed	66
Your Body	67
The Fishblood of a Woman	68
Pregnancy and Old Men	69
Aperture, *for Annie and Jim Wright*	71
Wake Me Up in a Hundred Years	72
A Woman's Buttocks, *for Virginia Woolf*	73
The Trees Are Dying	74
Answer to the Suicide	76
Shangri-la	77
The Lily Shivers	78
Woman from My Womb	79
Dancing Song for My Daughter, *after Gabriela Mistral*	80
Shaman's Song	81
As When Some Silenced Singer Hears Her Aria, *for Vittoria Colonna*	82
Through the "I" of the Needle	83

ABOUT THE AUTHOR 85

PART I: BLOOD AUTUMN

"The bloody massacre in Bangladesh quickly covered over the memory of the Russian invasion of Czechoslovakia, the assassination of Allende drowned out the groans of Bangladesh, the war in the Sinai Desert made People forget Allende, the Cambodian massacre made people forget Sinai, and so on and so forth until ultimately everyone lets everything be forgotten."

—Milan Kundera, *The Book of Laughter and Forgetting*

UNFINISHED AUTOBIOGRAPHY

I was born in 1941. The sky was falling.
The chairs of state
were arranging themselves in *"isms"* of death.
I learned to speak by fingering an apple,
rolling its crimson shine around in baby fingers,
because my mother's Slavic smile seemed to
give it onto the table of my highchair
in that Newark kitchen of new wintry mornings,
bright leaves at frosty windows just met
for the first time: autumn sun-
light, warm hands. *"God bless Mommy!*
God bless Daddy! God bless spaghetti!"
I chortled up to the big people
around my bedtime crib. When they laughed
I learned I had a pen for a tongue
that could please them.

Meantime, the bombs were falling,
the blitz began blitzing, Jewish, Polish flesh
sizzled in Hitler's ovens, lampshades of human skin,
gold fillings pulled from dead mouths
remade into wedding rings.
Are you wearing one? Has your gold
ring come from a mother's mouth
opened in mortified howl filled with poison gas
in the stifling chamber where she bled
menstrual blood down her thighs bereft of clothes,
crushing her child to her crowded breasts.

"Empathy" is my favorite word.
My peasant mother—war orphaned,
my lame Italian immigrant father,
"greenhorn guinea" they called him. *"Guinea gimp!"*
they shouted as he sold newspapers
for the state *"Education of the Poet"*

he gave to me, raising me in the ghetto of Newark
to speak good English where the worse that happened then
was when a boy named Herby chased me, cornering me
down the alley and kissed me,
sticking his tongue in my mouth,
choking me with mysterious sex as the other kids laughed:
"*Herby French-kissed Daniela!*" A grand joke
of the neighborhood. Nothing much else happened
until I was abused by a Klansman in a dark jail cell
one midnight, Sheriff of Montgomery County,
the only law for miles around Selma where
I integrated Deep South television as a journalist
announcing Freedom Rides and Sit-ins,
not out of bravery, but idealistic naivete.

Somewhere in between then and then,
I met a book full of rotting corpses,
photos of mutilated bodies on battlefields
or in concentration camps, dead faces distorted by screams,
dying hearts impaled on bayonets, and all my orgasms,
ever since have been screams of letting go of horrors
—guilty gaping skulls full of gold filled teeth.
I'm a *"Jersey girl"* who grew up, part Polish war orphan,
part Jew, half Italian immigrant
daughter of a lame *"guinea gimp,"* who was a poet dying
of the word, *"empathy,"* he carried on his back
and taught me Shakespeare's English.
He said I was too pretty for my own good
and read me Yeat's poem to his daughter,
but now I'm fifty-three, menopausal, insomniac,
and don't care much about looks. My greatest moment
of joy came in near death—not when I was jailed
by the Klansman Sheriff, but when I gave birth
to my daughter who came by emergency Caesarean,
bright with hope, lovely girl,
do you feel the ambulance siren of guilt,
grieving in your near death birth, the re-
birth of your mother and your moment of almost not
being new life greeting me in your eyes, my eyes
peering back at me, questioning, after the fever subdued.

Here's your crimson apple of being, daughter,
amidst new wars and books always repeating themselves
like autumn where death turns to beauty in dying leaves
singing their windy sighs
into the lies of hypocritical
histories of hand on reborn hand by hand murdered
and bleached to bones
or held warm or cold at fifty-three I can't sleep
well anymore. I grow fat eating love, I remember thrills
of my childhood autumns when the maples sang with sparrows
outside fall windows and the kitchen was warm as apples
turned crimson in pale hands—color of blood simply
being before I found the book of corpses
from ovens, battlefields, slave ships,
the ring of gold that broke in divorce
from your father whom I still love
and mourn. Now, I take you, daughter,
to the woods to meet the scarlet maples,
feed the wild deer, crush the leaves
and acorns with your steps, dance
in the moonlight, your mother is no orphan,
like hers was, your father is not lame like mine was,
but the Earth, Our Mother,
and all Her creatures swirl in clouds of gas, garbage, greed
the language of oppression: *"nigger, pollack, guinea, mick,
kike, jap, kraut, wasp, spick."*

Washington confronted its manufactured "Butcher of Baghdad"
and *"sand niggers"* were decried on Wall Street
where the banks collapsed in graft.
A tenuous thread of life secretes onto the page thickens
my eyes become someone else's. Are they yours, Daughter?
I collect a book on ethno-centricism, chemical,
biological, nuclear warfare and hate
the rich nuclear and oil barons who are your enemy.
We cannot live without enemies, Freud said,
but, these oil, nuclear, chemical, and germ warfare
profiteers hold us all hostage, you, me, and them,
to the screams of skulls with their forever gold

teeth, lampshades of human skin, their ears are ours
filled with a siren of guilt
from the history book of corpses, daughter.
It talks to autumn. It says: *"Empathize!"*
Because we all die to live
and eat and see and hold our crimson apple.

It's beauty makes us sing.

FOR GRANDMA LUCIA LA ROSA, "LIGHT THE ROSE"

> *"You're one of only two or three Italian-American women poets in this country, You're a pioneer. There are fewer of you known than Black or Puerto Rican women poets."*
>
> (Professor Ernesto Falbo, SUNY Buffalo, N.Y. 1976)

On the crowded subway,
riding to the prison to teach
Black and Puerto Rican inmates how to write,
I think of the fable of the shoemaker
who struggles to make shoes for the oppressed
while his own go barefoot over the stones.

I remember Grandma Lucia, her olive face
wrinkled with resignation,
content just to survive
after giving birth to twenty children,
without orgasmic pleasures or anesthesia.
Grandpa Galileo, immigrant adventurer,
who brought his family
steerage passage to the New World;
his shoemaker shop where he labored
over American factory goods
that made his artisan's craft a useless
anachronism; his Code of Honor
which forced him to starve
accepting not a cent of welfare
from anyone but his sons;
his ironic "Code of Honor"
which condoned jealous rages of wife-beating;
Aunt Elisabetta, Aunt Maria Domenica, Aunt Raffaella,
Aunt Elena, grown women huddled like girls
in their bedroom in Newark, talking in whispers,
not daring to smoke their American cigarettes
in front of *Pa*;

the backyard shrine of the virgin,
somber blue-robed woman,
devoid of sexual passions,
to whom Aunt Elisabetta prayed
daily before dying in childbirth,
trying to have *"a son"*
against doctor's orders, though
she had five healthy daughters already;
Dr. Giuseppe Ferrara, purple heart veteran
of World War II, told he couldn't have a residency
in a big New York hospital because of his Italian
name; the Mafia jokes, the epithets:
"Wop, guinea, dago, grease-ball."
And the stories told by Papa
of Dante, Galileo, Da Vinci, Marconi, Fermi, Caruso
that stung me with pride for Italian *men*;
how I was discouraged from school,
told a woman meant for cooking and bearing
doesn't need education.

I remember
Grandma
got out of bed
in the middle of the night
to fetch her *husband* a glass of water
the day she died,
her body wearied
from giving and giving and giving
food and birth.

AMERICAN SONNETS FOR MY FATHER

> *—for Donato Gioseffi 1906-1981—*
> *written in Edna St. Vincent Millay's studio*
> *at Steepletop, New York, November, 1981*

You died in spring, father, and now the autumn dies.
Bright with ripe youth, dulled by time,
plums of feeling leaked red juices from your eyes,
pools of blood hemorrhaged in your quivering mind.
At forty, I climb Point Pinnacle, today,
thinking of you gone forever from me.
In this russet November woods of Millay,
I wear your old hat, Dear Italian patriarch, to see
if I can think you out of your American grave
to sing your unwritten song with me.
Your poetry, love's value, I carry with your spirit.
I take off your old black hat and sniff at it
to smell the still living vapor of your sweat.

You worked too hard, an oldest child of too many,
a lame thin boy in ragged knickers, you limped
all through the 1920s up city steps, door to door
with your loads of night and daily newspapers, each worth
a cheap labored penny of your family's keep.
You wore your heart and soles sore. At forty,
not climbing autumn hills like me, you lay with lung disease
strapped down with pain and morphine, hearing your breath
rattle in your throat like keys at the gates of hell.
Your body was always a fiend perplexing your masculine will.
You filled me with pride and immigrant tenacity. Slave
to filial duty, weaver of all our dreams, you couldn't be free
to sing. So be it. You are done, unfulfilled by song except in me.
If your dreams are mine, live again, breathe in me and be.

You never understood America's scheme.
Your wounded dream, father,

will never heal in me, your spirit mourns forever
from my breath, aches with childhood memory,
sighs for my own mortality in you,
which I, at last accept
more completely than ever when we
laughed together and seemed we'd go on forever—
even though we always knew
you would die much sooner than I
who am your spirit come from you.
Remember, *"a father lost, lost his!"* you told us,
preparing us with Shakespearean quotation
and operatic feeling for your inevitable death.

Good night, go gently, tired immigrant father
full of pride and propriety. We, your
three daughters, all grew
to be healthier, stronger, more American than you.
Sensitive father, I offer you this toast,
no empty boast, "I've never known a man braver!"
The wound that will not heal in me
is the ache of dead beauty.
Once full of history, philosophy, poetry,
physics, astronomy, your bright, high flying psyche
is now dispersed, set free from your tormented body,
but the theme you offered, often forlorn,
sheer luminescent soul, glistened with enough light
to carry us all full grown.

GUILT IS A GIFT THAT IS GIVEN

Guilt is a gift that is given
to love, a wound in the heart
that says there is duty,
the message in the blood of family,
as to the father and mother
of duty is born the child of duty
and to the sisters and brothers
their name together
shared in home,
a place the spirit retreats to
when the world is cold and dark
and hunger stalks the woods.

Blood is thick and red
and should not spill like water
on silent rock.
My blood is given to the trees
as I fall on my knees, alone,
to you, father, who taught me filial duty,
and all your kin have forsaken me
Like you, I am Lear, alone on the heath
with only one Cordelia,
the one you said I resembled,
and I've been given one daughter
who carries your blood, but not your name
which I've given the fame of duty.

THE GIRL WITH PURPLE HAIR

wears a black leather jacket full of safety pins and leans
on crutches. Her legs are mangled and her friend
looks anorexic in black tights which show her thin legs.
Both have beautiful faces, lost looks, eyes sunken in.
They seem like runaways and disembark the subways
at notorious 42nd Street where pimps and dens of inequity
have reigned through the century
of whores and drug dealers dressed like rock stars
of heavy metal bands. *"Bad Brains, Circle Jerks, Jonny Rotten,"*
who was, and murdered his girlfriend.

Up and down the halls of the colleges, I hear
the children "Mother F-ing'" this and that
as they go cursing everything up and down
the escalators and elevators and back again.
In bus terminals and in trains, leather-jacketed kids
pretend to be tough, their green, purple, blue dyed
hair, depressed faces, hollow stare.

One girl's legs seem gnarled with birth defects,
the others are too thin to stand on.
You've seen them, too, and worried about them as I do,
as you fret over the global heat trap, ozone layer,
nuclear waste dumps, biological warfare tests,
Savings and Loan scandals,
dying economy, polluted land and groundwaters, crack
in the ghettos and cocaine on Wall Street, death squads
in El Salvador, Haiti, Bosnia, rape and rising taxes,
unemployment up with your job down on the line, crumbling
roads and subways, falling bridges, plutonium
shot into space on rockets! And so you let them go,
let them pass away from you as I do,
knowing they won't make it far into old age
like me at fifty-three worried about my heart
and high cholesterol, knowing my grandchildren,

if I have them, may be as doomed as these lost,
vulnerable, tough, black leather-jacketed children
full of safety pins, purple haired and anorexic. I remember
how hard my immigrant father worked
to take himself out of rags
and see how hard these kids work to wear them.

Caught in my throat,
I feel their anger
sharp
as a starved
shin bone.

THE PRACTICAL NURSE

is neatly dressed in slacks
and clearly Black,
strong legged and a little fat.
On her right arm an old grey woman leans pale
and small and frail, bird boned, clearly white
and Jewish. They are on their way
to the country house of the stroke victim's son,
no doubt. The old able-bodied Black woman
is a practical nurse, I surmise from her blank
but steady eyes, now the daily mate,
constant companion of an older white woman. They
are more together, day
in and out, than all
their children, husbands or friends.
You might say they are married and walk
like a bride and groom through the gloom
of the Port Authority Bus Station.
The work of the Black nurse comforts and frees
the children of the stroke victim, but leaves
the children she feeds
alone. Who will walk with her when she's old,
and will she manage to grow old
enough to need a nurse
or afford one?

THE THUMBLESS BUS DRIVER

Takes my ticket with his missing thumb, just enough
of a stub remains to rest
the small card in the crease
where his thumb should fold into his hand.

I think of my nephew with his hand caught
in an antique car fan, four fingers severed
and sewn on again, stiff forever. And old Uncle Joe
who survived the *Battle of the Bulge*
in World War II, only to have his fingers crushed
in an assembly line when he placed an aluminum sheet
inside a machine that pressed it into pie plates. How his face
must have paled at the sight of his fingers
mashed to bloody pulp.
He never really smiled again, and went on to marry a cruel
and homely woman who gave him one good son
and more misery after that.
We never really knew if World War II or pies brought his demise.

I have a friend who is blind since birth
and walks and rides the subway to work
everyday in New York City. No "seeing eye" dog,
just her white cane leads her way.
And we who see are afraid of what lurks in dark alleys.

I remember the tale of a magician told by a gnomish Irish wit,
about a trickster who performed slight of hand wonders
with a missing index on his right hand
never noticed by his audience
thoroughly engrossed by his dextrous tricks.

I remember my father, long dead, who
with lame and shortened leg, learned to ride a bicycle, hop
on a pogo stick, dance the Tango at Arthur Murray's Studio,
like all of us, unwilling to be labeled
as less than the best endurance of his test.

The thumbless bus driver's lost finger shows
like a wound in his eyes—
though he drives well and takes tickets with his missing
thumb. How could he take them with his good left hand
when the entrance to the bus is on his right?

THE MOTHER AT THE ZOO

looks as if she has been struck dumb.
Being a Black woman in the South Bronx
is difficult enough,
but having a child like this!
Still, she wheels
him dutifully through the zoo
in his chair, his long arms
and full grown legs
all askew, his head gently
pillowed wobbling
to one side
his crippled hand
bent to his cheek,
dazed eyes stare
at the trees above—
he does not speak
or request ice cream,
lollipops or views
of the giraffe or lion,
balloons or pizza.
He requires only her patience,
and her love dazes her
as if she were numbed by his birth.

Does she wonder why or has she stopped
asking? I can see
only patience in her eyes,
the kind
that crosses over despair
to resignation
and does not ask
only bears
"Why?"

THE BLIND SOPRANO SINGS

—for Cheryl Taylor

Slow sensual openings happen in the concert hall,
eyes, pupils, irises, lilies, leaves, heart valves,
moist mouths, silk sleeves, flags, words unfurled
and feelings far beyond their meanings
as we listen and the blind soprano changes
the pain of this dark terror, this inscrutable mystery
we live into bright sound, sensed sublimity,

Cantatas, concerti, canons,
contain captured passions
from centuries before, still sing:
have pity human heart on human heart.

Leaves absorb light, shed shades of green wonder, color,
string, bow, dance, breath of the blind soprano's spirit
heralded by cornet, cello, violin,
viola, big base viol, all played by women
diaphanously clothed in pale flesh, yellow chiffon frills,
she fingers Braille notes, translates touch to sound
notes from the dark chambers in her head, echoing
harmony spreads smiles on the blind soprano's lips, sonorous
sound swells triumphant in the loss of sight;
her trills thrill tears, awe from my eyes over-full
with seeing as I feel
your dear hand dance
rhythmic touch on my shoulder.

JAZZ LADY OF THE SUBWAY

She sings her heart out with a smile
like Louis Armstrong on the subway's dusty platform
with her band, a base, guitar, horn player,
and drummer. She keeps singing with a smile
even as an old demented man dances up and down,
keeping rhythm in front of her, blocking the audience view,
with his big rag of a coat, swollen leg and crutch.
Undaunted, smiling even at the old beggar who steals her
spotlight. *"Music Under New York"* says her sign, and she's among
the good jazz musicians who play in the subways for quarters
and dollars collected in a hat or instrument case open
in front of them.
Making music amidst the rumble of trains and rush of people
who are made more cheerful by their tunes.
Evelyn Blakey knows that the homeless man
who dances on his crutch is comforted by her warble.
*"Georgia, Georgia . . . just an old sweet tune keeps Georgia
on my mind . . ."* he sings along with her, grinning soul,
the sort of smile that says: "I've been
through it all, but sing anyway." Evelyn Blakey, listens
to the horn jam, listens to the drums roll,
with ecstatic eyes closed, face full of music,
and the old beggar dances on his swollen foot,
his ragged coat swings back and forth with his tired bones,
his grey head bobs in rhythm,
and Evelyn, Evelyn, Evelyn Blakely sings,
her heart full of sonorous sound,
her foot tapping the ground,
her subway commuters gather around.

AESCHYLUS CHORUS

> *It's the end of the century;*
> *almost everyone dreams of money or revenge.*
> —Stephen Dunn

From the stone towers of glass eyes,
ears clogged with grey smoke,
fingers numbed by the Atlantic's winter winds,
we unhouse our homeless heads, under fierce
skies, merciless sun. While political stooges
ply your votes in our shadows
pushing your hearts
with the stigmata of promises
to house or starve us, the untaxable throng
who defecate on your doorsteps.

You'd rather hear good jokes and happy tunes,
and who can blame your rejecting
our grubby faces or paws always there
thrust out at your comfortable walk.
You want to go gingerly as if
we're barnacles on your pavement.
We wait with tremulous breath
at the end of your line.
We stink up your commute.
The very rich never see us through the
darkened windows of their limousines,
sleek, dazzling, chauffeured, sipping cocktails
on cellular phones.

Only you, the workers of the city
who rush to your unbearable jobs
steam past us in guilt,
an umbilicus connecting our lives to yours
in ghastly communion
that squeezes your breath.

Our breath is already drawn
like an over exposed x-ray.
We take no bite of your body.
We're too weak to steal your watch
or briefcase. We live in bottles
and broken boxes on subway grates
and sleep sick to death in
your dark doorways.
We drink the hot salt of our own dry sweat,
wash our underwear in your park fountains,
and dreams and wishes no longer hiss
through our nights as we take up your benches.
We can't afford tears. They would spread like our lice
and tuberculosis and drown you everywhere,
workers, New Yorkers. Go on your way,
there is nothing between us.
Let the politicos ply your votes
with false promises to house or starve us.

ON TOP OF THE EMPIRE STATE

New York City of money as God at the top
of your TV tower power,
beaming out over the New Jersey of my birth in
Passaic County, kid I once was from an Italian ghetto
of Newark, and Little Falls near Paterson—
I view GE, UN, Brooklyn Bridge, World Trade Center,
Macy's, PAN-AM, Seagrams, Gothic turrets of *Capitalismo*,
machismo, city of stone towers, concrete walks
racing up and down Park Avenue. Tourists from everywhere
up here to see you—German, French, Arabic, Italian,
Spanish et cetera tongues lapping and wagging up
thick air pollution, yellow cabs
like toy cars below. City of Gothic aspiration,
city of death and poetry,
city of telephone wires nibbled by rats and garbage.
City I longed to come to as a girl from New Jersey,
near suburban Paterson. I used to view you
from Garett Mountain where we necked as teenagers.
A lovers' lane lost in memory as I face your clock towers
rising higher than your churches, your trees are dwarfs
amidst the concrete turrets
where smoke rises from air conditioners
and incinerators cough up your ethnic hatreds—
while down in your streets
people scurry exchanging stocks, money, bad goods,
satellite dishes whirl with signals,
police and ambulance sirens cut
the hum of gassy vibrations, King Kong climbs up to die
and fall his black fur bloody with the glass knives
of your squared eyes upon billions of windows and lips sealed
in agony of the African-American who dies
in the promise and lies
of your dusty sunlit and sunless streets.
Autumn colors rust red and yellow of your patch of Park,
central navel where trees and lakes bloom

in your altered air, city of the flat-topped Twin Towers,
of phallic clichéd greed city of many-cultured people,
city of money and books, poetry and music, Jews, Haitians,
Puerto Ricans, Africans, Italians, Chinese, Koreans, Swedes,
French, Japanese, Irish, Polish tourists of the Empire City of glass
and stone, asphalt, concrete and brick, city of the Empire prick
of Gothic greed of white man's tart taste of every restaurant
cuisine art of Manhattan, Yorkshire, new again,
city of the Dutch Englishman, stolen rock of the red man—
indigenous owner of you, native dying under your erection,
where shells are gone from your river waters flowing,
under legs of steel bridges thrown over your voluptuous waters,
East river flow, Hudson Valley polluted with PCBs
spilling on my New Jersey, your smoke and garbage,
from GE's bomb builders multinational headquarters
of death dealers water tanks on the tops of all
your buildings robbed of their sea breezes,
Atlantic nibbling at your sandy beaches,
rock-cracking vibrations with the weight of your tonnage,
ape at your tower, rape of the black heart,
City of the Duke of York,
city of RCA, CBA, UN, GE, AIDS, PAN-AM, TIME-LIFE,
McGraw Hill, Paramount, Random House Inc. ink, oink,
oink, oink brilliant pig city, of honking horns and coins
and quartered views, Yankee
Stadium baseball Mets of the Metropolis,
multi-billion dollar baseball opiate of suffering earth
cavernous Chrysler-scape of land rape by George Washington
Bridge to Welfare Island skyport navy yard of nuclear
nucleus warhead godhead, Queensboro of the Kingsboro
burrowed, Big Apple
rock, stolen from Indians, and roll of the Atlantic port
waters of the Statue of Liberty
holding a lantern aloft to cheap immigrant laborer
refugees of World Wars, I, II, and now III here in our genes
with radiation, shadow of World Trade Towers Empire
of Hollywood's King Kong monster heart growls
in the guilt of Gothic churches
of the money god city of Broadway a glitter gog, a goggle glee
dubbed with songster Romance of Jews and Christians, Neo-Nazi

swastikas on synagogues and Catholic Churches
from the New Aryan Nation,
KKK skinheads, of the heavy-metal generations
of the rock and roll harbor—city of hot dogs and dogs
who are too hot, ice-cream cones melting souvenirs
of stuffed King Kong toys with red tongues and red bow ties
and angry black crossed eyes of liberty's lies of ape
in love with blond doll, rape of the heart of Africa
come full circle round the island and see the harbor view
at sunset behind the Verrazzano arch of suspension the Twin Towers
of might and TV radio power, bomb-shaped turrets of rock
peninsula thrust out into the great Atlantic mystery of might
international city of *"get thee behind me devil,"*
city of muggers and sluggers, crack city of cocaine dreams
of fat women longing to be too thin of fin and fun
of spire and liar, aspiration of iron lady and wounded man
of raped mother earth and brick swords sky scraping
greedy city of darkness and darkening people,
of ozone and whole in the sky pie in the eye, pill in the gill,
comedian city, of Vaudeville,
corpus corps of Empire power trotting stones trapped in entropy
New Yorker from New Jersey, me, of Brooklyn, New Jersey
turnpike flower child of Ike and Nixon and Kennedy
"Ask not . . . do for your country," Madison Square Garden
of cameras clicking from your observation deck. Observed city
of subterranean paths and heliported roofs.
City City City of the nuclear and oil baron's
dollars exchanged for yen
of copper wires and ventilator, elevator shafts!
I scoff at you and celebrate you. I mock and marvel
at you, *ai, oh, eeah, ow, oi* and *ouh, yoh, wow*!
and rush fast talking city my home. I roam
up to the Gothic elevated top of you and stare
in the face of your clocks speeding up
in geological time, rock of rocks, canyons of greed, glass
of glassy, classy Park Avenue Fifth Avenue views. Here I am,
the Italian, Polish, Jewish, Albanian, New Yorker
from Passaic County, New Jersey,
born in Newark, reared in Paterson,
whose father came through

The Island of Tears in your harbor.
Phooey on you! I'm going home to New
Jersey,
back to Little Falls,
back to Paterson
again,
and then up to Sussex County
to spend my last years
full of the tears and sardonic laughter
of knowing and loving you.
Look for the name *"Gioseffi,"* near *Ginsberg*,
on your immigrant's wall at Ellis Island,
City of my poets' pain and tears and joy!

I marvel and mock you. I hate and love you,
throbbing wonder
my head and heart all blown asunder
at the high view of you from your sleek
turret central to your Empire's view
you've
broken
my Jersey soul in two
and taught me
everything and nothing
Neeeeeew
Yooork!

CENTO AT DAWN

The wind blows out of the gates of the day.
Let the night keep what the night takes away,
dreamt in a dream the heavy soul, somewhere
struck suddenly and dark down to its knees,
sighs as a griffon sighs off in the orphic air—
awakes as morning at the brown brink eastward springs
and the whole landscape flushes on a sudden at a sound—
the clang of waking life; the streets are stirred,
      birds fly to the glistening roofs and sing;
an omnibus across the bridge
      crawls like a yellow butterfly,
while I stand on the roadway and on the pavement grey
and dream that beauty passes like a dream
      fastened to a dying animal.

Cento is an Italian form of verse in which lines and refrains from poets of the past are deliberately used and combined into a new poem.

BLOOD AUTUMN

Memory of autumn, of menopausal bleeding,
and the blood from a creature you hunted
in the autumn woods oozed over a wet rock,
you used as a table in the brook,
carving the meat from the bone,
skinning it down to naked flesh I squatted
behind a stump, shuddering at the death
I'd seen, crying secretly as I peed and bled
into the dying and wondrous leaf soaked earth.
I'd wanted to go with you,
in this awful autumn of aging, I'd said I go
bird watching with binoculars
as you hunted with your shotgun.
I was tired of my girlish squeamishness,
of worries of bombs poised in silos,
germ warfare bred in laboratories,
chemicals stirred to deadly alchemies, genius death,
a lump flowering, a cancer blooming in my left breast
to be removed next week by the surgeon's laser knife
all in the hope of flesh
how the deer trembled to its death
first day of hunting season
fattened against winter from summer's gathering,
nibble by nibble of wild berry, young shoots,
lichen and wild fruit—only to fall
in a leap over the swell of forest floor,
into our dell crunching leaves, a flurry like the explosive
dive made by the osprey as it splashes into the lake
to seize a fish from on high. Suddenly,
there in the quiet gully of noon, leaves rustled,
twigs cracked as the deer ran toward us, seated silently
in wait, sounds squirrel chatters, bird chirps quieted down
from our alien intrusion of the woods bleeding red
oak and yellow maple, beech leaves carpeting
the floor of cathedrals, trees' gothic in their reach heavenward

toward dazzling blue sky. Camouflaged by bark, she leapt
into our gully
where your shotgun was poised beyond all
my arguments against its cruel blasted noise.
   "From the beginning of time, men have hunted!"
This is how I stay in touch with reality.
When the secret police come for your family,
you want them to have the only weapons?
A man has to know how to survive. To hunt as he's hunted!"

Terror everywhere in the global heat trap,
puppets of oil and nuclear barons
elected by advertisements for more profits.
Homeless dying in the streets of our city
while Turks were driven from Bulgaria,
Armenians killed in Russia, Hungarians
murdered in Rumania, indigenous people everywhere
destroyed in apartheid systems, the Philippines stolen
from Filipinos, El Salvador from Salvadorans,
as Haiti's rain forests were chopped to dust
and an Iranian and PAN AM jet crashed
like fallen deer into a gully killing your son
as this doe fled another hunter's gun, flew into
our murderous view and I shouted, *"There!"*
and you spun around and fired
into this bleeding autumn turned
to glorious color—
dying leaves fallen to fertilize
the next coming of leaves
back into roots of bleeding trees
like me, bleeding too much as I grow old
and matronly, thinking of him—
your young son gone forever
on his college semester in Europe
into oblivion—
gone amidst the garbage of greed about to backfire
as shotguns that kill the killers holding them.
But, your aim was accurate, your gun well kept,
you shot the doe, bagged it, the first time
I'd seen you kill,

though I knew you'd got deer before
and in winter wild boar
fried squirrels and possums since you were a boy
escaping alone into the wild where
your Jewish father, a Turkish immigrant, wanted you to learn
to survive, defend yourself: *"A man
must be a man to be a man!"* he'd said,
and I was tired of arguing non-violence
to you and the rest of the warring world.
With my bird watching binoculars,
I'd joined you in the hunt
and saw the deer coming toward us,
my eyes and ears sharper than your fading ones.
I wanted you at seventy to win, to feel young again,
as the week before you'd lain
in an emergency ward
needing a transfusion. You'd bled
too much from your aging gut. "Acute diverticulosis,
an ailment of old men," the doctor said
and sent you to your hospital bed.
I wanted you to feel strong. Your hand
squeezed the trigger
and the doe fell, trembling
and I covered my ears
and unexpected tears stung my eyes
as I watched you fire again
to finish the quivering animal—
a second shot to the temple, meat
for the winter of your seventieth year.

While you carved, I peed blood into the red leaves
and listened to the starlings rustling the branches,
the sparrows chirp in the brush, your knife
on stone, carved
the doe into meat, all her intricate muscles bled,
her beautiful eyes stilled, her graceful head
a trophy for a wall, her skin to be tanned
into leather boots and gloves, her ribs exposed
like our vulnerable hearts pumping
until they stop soon. Beyond this autumn

the laser knife of a brilliant and self-destructive technocracy
will carve my breast, remove a tumor
to determine if time is benign,
and if it is,
I will cook for you
the delicate, gamey venison
which I won't taste,
as I eat less and less meat
and you grow old tasting the hunt,
controlling death by giving it and I give into it
bleeding more heavily than ever in my youth,
as I grow beyond the years of fecund mothering—
our different ways of facing death,
your fight against it, giving it, my giving into it,
the power I can't possess of gun, or knife, or cock-
sure ways.

I wept like a squeamish girl
seeing the deer tremble
and your old hands trembling, too, as you carved
its heart out and I knew that you
are hurt by your own necessity,
saddened like me by blood autumn,
her shimmering beauty.

PART II: ANIMAL INTIMACIES

The future of religion
is in the mystery of touch.

—D. H. Lawrence

AFTER OUR ARGUMENT, WE CANOE

peacefully on the lake to see what we might sight,
some exciting species of wild life
for our list of wondrous things we've seen since spring
and there before us on the high limbs of a russet sugar maple,
ablaze with October sun, beside a burnished,
crimson Chestnut Oak,
sits a flock of Turkey Vultures,
red headed with hooked, black buzzard beaks, they pose
before rays of morning sun, wings spread to preen and bathe
away vermin from under the their wing pits. Black feathers bask
in iridescent hue. These ancient birds were sacred to Egyptians,
carrion cleaners of the woods, eaters of the sacrificial entrails
of deer, sheep or lamb, bear or rat, swallowers of wasted flesh
who never kill to eat, but simply make the dead fly
from the rotting earth, soar toward the sky,
taking dead souls heavenward.

Holy birds, Black Vultures
who can make the carrion flesh of the dead
rise again into the autumn sky ahead,
you who never prey on the living or kill as we
and the mighty hawks or eagles do,
carrion eaters, big black buzzards of the blooming autumn,
please fly with my dead spirit to the tallest trees,
bask my soul in sun, bless my pain with fun
of soaring free, run with me heavenward flapping flying,
sailing on the wind amidst the flutter of colors and sun
mixed in every hue and mood, bring me to your forest roost,
tell me all the secrets of night so that I might
not fear the rotting purple and blue flesh we all become
when blood autumn finally leaves our view and we lie dormant
as the trees in an eternal springless dormancy!
Black birch dead upon the ground, I gather your debris
to light the fire and make my home blaze with the warmth
of your death in the hearth. Tree, once a thing of beauty

that I burn the way a buzzard sails on wind,
nurtured by the dead turned to carrion, heal me, let me learn
to love my impatient husband again after our cruel fight,
and let my soul fly with the birds above the glass still lake
wherein the sleek fish eat and mate.

RETURNING FROM PARADISE WE STOP AT A CARNIVAL

and view the "freaks"
watching us, and offer a smile
to the snake charmer. She nods at us
       knowing we are lovers returning from paradise.
At night, just before dawn of the last day
of an old year, we have a common nightmare.
Each falls asleep and wakes alone
in a dream on a cold shore
far from home, without shelter from wind, sun
       dark, cold, heat.
I feel like a tiny breathing thing alone in a vast night
no hand anywhere to hold mine. I call to you, friend,
brother, lover, husband, but you can't answer
out of your body, alone in your dream crying for friend,
sister, lover wife!

We wake into life
sure of dying under the frozen sky
and mute stars, glistening with winter light.
We have returned from paradise and visited a carnival
many times again, to view the "freaks" watching us
and smile at the knowing snake charmer.
Sometimes, as we look at the pain in the other's eyes
each recalls the nightmare had separately,
but we do not speak of it. We hold hands into new years,
knowing all new years turn old, and listen to the night,
snow creaking in mounds, and the air iced from the Northwind.

For the sake of the other
we do not say
how each together
is alone
returning from paradise.

SHEEPDOG OF THE CITY

I'm your nurse because the doctors
wear penises. I'm Scarlet O'Hara
wearing an ancient Chinese mask at your
funeral. Yesterday, I looked into
the mirror and your scars
were on my face. I call to you
because fathers disembowel children
as a ritual to war gods. I call to you
because dart throwers chase me
through a circus of elevators
and orphans wander
wounded by madness in the streets,
asking for my last slice of bread.

I'm the Whore of Babylon
sucking your love,
pulling weeds from your throat.
I'm the sheepdog wandering in your dreams,
the white cane tapping away your blindness.
My breasts are sensitive to the rain
because I listened to the rain with you.

TOWARD THE GREATER ROMANCE,
PLEASE PLACE ROSES IN MY SKULL:
A Tantric Love Song

Oh my love, I will carry
your lantern ahead,
whispering light for your steps.
Please touch me to come to you.

Toward the light, Father, Mother,
shining harbor ahead,
all grievance closed on our breasts,
sound coloring words to breath.

Glide with me through my river.
I've come this way, too,
slithering out as new flesh.
Our bodies burst into bloom.

Hands know silk, skin and petals,
wet mouth, apple's breath.
Place roses into my skull.
Our bones are white, pupils black.

Oh my love, shine with my life,
be as my brother,
yin and *yang* flowing bright milk
from autumn leaves in the grass.

Oceans swirl, marble blue earth,
hear, taste, feel, see, heal,
toward the explosion of light,
eyes opening souls from death.

THE RUBY THROATED HUMMINGBIRDS ARE GONE

They've flown south now
and one Great Egret fishes the pond
as Broadwinged Hawks begin their migrations,
kenneling on thermal currents of wind
off above yellowing mountains.
Now, Snakeweed blooms along the trail choking
white and purple Asters. A few bleeding
leaves fall amidst wilting greenery. Poison
Ivy turns red with warning.

My eighty-three-year-old mother still argues
with my father, twelve years dead. Their hatred
reverberates in a back room
of my head, rattling memories of my lonely childhood.
Their loathing for each other
colors all my days with pain. I loved him
because he loved me best, but I look like her,
my face and spirit tear
at each other.
I am the child of hate.

A wounded love sprouts like a weed
from watery depths,
uncultivated,
flowers, white and purple, bloom,
even in these days of dying
leaves.

Beyond winter,
no one
grieves.

WINTER DARK

Over frozen rocks, water flows,
"like time" poets say. Time, the only thawed thing in this
grey winter dark. Our lake is ice
and I have come at fifty-three to a quiet dutiful life.
You, older than I, have lost your strength
to arthritis. Pain killers have numbed you
and your passionate nature waxes like the moon.
Hypertension's therapeutic drug makes you drowsy, too.
Beyond the horizon, there's all ice and snow.
I crunch on through the dormant woods,
leaving the icy lake behind, and you,
reading in our warm bed full of books.

Here fallen Eastern Hemlocks killed by Asian blight
lie cracked across forbidden ice. Their pedestals, drip dry pine
needles on the frozen snow.

No, not even a vulture
climbs the horizon of barren trees.
I'm on my knees without God for a crutch, just the wondrous science
of relentless cycles of seasons, new life from decay and carrion.
A few crows cackle and caw above, a welcome sign of vitality.
I have a dear daughter grown into her own love and work,
an aged mother to whom I feel undying duty,
I have my work ahead and that is all. The lake is frozen cold, no
fish leap or stir in her. Even the flock of vultures who lived above
her warming their wings in fall, sunning lice away, have strayed
to another lake. Nothing rides a thermal, nothing flies or stirs
on the horizon all is dull and grey.
I crunch on through the frozen snow.
I do not even dream of spring.
I listen to the laughter of departing crows.
Time the only thawed thing flows
over the icy rocks and streams
into the woods until somewhere longer,

farther than I can go it finds the ocean,
where it loses its deltas to become
part of a churning entropic universe
too vast to know.

BENEATH THE DREAMING TREE

Oh God, or Goddess, make me a child again
beneath the dreaming tree where leaves drop golden
sunlight all around me
in a fantasy of benevolent faith
which extols itself in *"Thee."*

Now, no answers come from above
or below.
Silence sings in my aging cranium—
throbbing like Prospero's
to let loose infinity.
Eternity embraces entropy.

"We are to blame
for the blood that flows from wounds."
says love as it glows red from the bled heart
under the hanging tree.

A fairy land of angels, gods and goddesses
cavorts in mythologies or legends old as Gilgamesh,
answering from the brain as it talks to itself,
right to left, left to right lobe,
each one of us is alone on the vast globe
doomed to dust or carrion.
Even in the best touch of skin to another's within,
each is alone
with conscience in search of piety
which comes easily in old age
when the animal appetite
is done with the flesh
and longs to escape
body into pure mind,
as if there were a God or Goddess
who were kind enough
to embrace the perfect zero
we become
when we're done with breath
and animal flesh meets animal death.

THE LANGUAGE OF LIGHT

—for my dying wandering Angus

I try to sing so that our scars will glisten
as crystal goblets full of purple grapes
we raise to our lips, our last supper
on Earth we'll share as communion:
bounty of blue water, black earth, afloat
in silence except for our stammering
before She passes into the past
sizzled by fire or ice our shimmering
nerves cling together on the edge
of threatened futures. The past is
eternal only to lovers.

I want to sing to you in a language
of light bright as feathers, hope,
alone in my skin tonight,
sings as it falls in slivers
of light through air as rain in my sight
and my heart wells in my throat
as a bird struggles
against a night predator
and darkness presses over it.

We worry if our children will live to speak
a language of light and sing to their children
of silver apples of night,
golden apples of day,
each must gather wandering over green meadows
where daises or wild violets spring,
blooming gloriously to death beside brooks,
streams froth and tumble dreams
from nooks and crannies, run
over rocks, secret forest places where dear deer
nibble wild blueberries, or lions stalk

blood from the language of light. My incessant hope
tastes tongues of light; my arms will hold you
safely in the night, until time
in time
is done.

SUNLIGHT

shines, at last!
Spring will come again.
It's an old song, you say.
But I say
the heart must learn it anew.

Now Chickadees and Titmice
peck amidst the winter berries
and pines.
Soon the Rubythroated Hummingbird will flit
among honeysuckle blooms,
a new calf will be born
in the barn on the hill

and a pregnant doe
will nibble my crocuses
before they're full.

APRIL LOON

One lone Loon glides along the lake.
Lost from a mate,
she wears a smart suit of black tweed,
checkered and flecked with white.
Her black dagger beak poised
to spear a silvery fish
as she dives deep to hide
from the Canada Goose who swims too near.

After a long wait
she surfaces far off.
Ancient heavy boned bird,
different from all the rest,
superb diver, odd singer, like you,
I sing my weird tune, loony with the beauty of spring,
rebirth amidst the fears of a weakened heart. Blood
circulates poorly now as wrinkles prepare me
to want less of life.

Little peach beak of the Goldfinch, yellow as my Forsythia bush
which droops its fountains of bright blossoms over the walk,
crimson cardinal flower and bird, sun rise
and sunset of natural color, wonder of Earth,
amazing bright green and yellow visions of thawing woods,
it *is* enough that April has come again
like an idiot babbling and strewing flowers, April
the *kindest* month,
reminding me it's enough
to live like a lonely loon lost
on a cool lake, just to see the Bank Swallows swoop,
the iridescent Tree Swallow sail across the azure sky,
the Barn Swallows leap up with the loon's cry, loony loon am I,
lost on the lake, time a threat now as I call my last cries
over the water—violins in my ears! Sing, gold
and red raspberry finches, Song Sparrows, white throated
ones, too, and Wood or Hermit Thrush, sing

your sweet tunes, sound your small flutes
while I laugh like a loon
lost in dandelion wine, lost in Wood Anemone,
searching for the Wood Ducks who shyly fly, white wing stripes
on a dark silhouetted sky, high and higher,
no clumsy flyer like the dinosaur loon,
lost in its own wild and plaintive tune.

Tap of Downy Woodpecker,
laughing song of the Northern Flicker,
sweet throated Yellow Warbler, Mourning Dove,
tiny Black Capped Chickadee, Grey Tufted Titmouse,
sing to me, whistle away, fill my day with lazy wonder.
I'm tired of diving down and rising up
to gulp a silvery fish. I want to float, heavy
boned on the deep water, no waves, no wind,
only gentle balmy ripples of spring.
I can't grieve the bombs that could be trees,
the children that didn't come from me,
those who have not lived or died too soon,
let me fall on my knees in the grass
and sleep in the meadow on an old deer path.

Sing to me loony Common Loon
tunes, laugh a nocturnal laugh, of how the last
first green of life, the last noon of sun,
the last glimpse of light,
matters!

THE PREGNANT GARDENER

A pregnant woman gardens, naked in her glass greenhouse.
Plants she tends and water grow from her fingers,
green silhouettes against her full belly;
round in the moonlight, a rapture
flows through her breasts to the mouth of a child,
containing all melody,
while father-starved boys
in dark cellars of crowded cities
slam-dance to anti-music made of nuclear explosions.

Earth hemorrhages Her plush wealth, bloody bombs
phallic shaped from wheatless silos,
prisoners of peace
accurately aimed
hate fail-safe or fail-deadly force
opposite to love, to eyes kissed,
bread baking in warm kitchens,
babies at nippled breasts,
suckled on green leaves which rise serene
from muddy earth, wet with animal dreams
as our human hands
in these dark times
touch bliss.

THE GUILLOTINE AND THE CATHEDRAL

—for Alejo Carpentier

The missile like a final guillotine of a man's world
stands erect against immense history—
a red and purple sun
sets as the scent of orange flowers
excites the wind.
Giant waves, powerful
Greek tragedies, drum rolls
greet ears like shells
filled with the voice of the executioner
as he reads his list
to the crowd and trees tremble;
big continents protrude like butterfly wings,
flutter in the atmosphere of blue seas
swirling in drifts and currents
as they cling to Earth's surface
as She spins amidst women's wails
and birthings.
The cathedral explodes
with organ music by Bach and Haydn
and a machine-gun in the rhythym of Lohengren
grinds blood from the passers by
who are surprised to die
in the middle of the priest's sermon.
Chaos like a riot of birds
chatters over the bridge
to the other side of nowhere
until a fragile child small and wild
weeps her way, shoving through the crowds of the dead
who have come to witness their own execution.
She peeps out bleary eyed from between the bloody legs
of the woman who sells refreshments to survive
and with her innocent eyes
enchants all meanings into place
like a rose garden full of trellises and cakes.

THE SIGN OF THE CROSS

—for Gertrude Stein

Because of the cat's eye marble of your passion,
you old sage of roses, I slap my hand
on your big rump, old word whore!
You discovered the secrets of your body
only to keep them silent to the grave.

You contemporary of my late Italian grandmother
whose cadaver appears before me in my dreams,
her clitoris gleaming like a ruby jewel—
grandma who gave birth to *twenty* children
alone in her bed, her own midwife. Grandma
who never knew the numbing power of orgasmic
potency, pool of cosmic energy
for the tormented body.

For you, Dear Grandma, and for you, Ole Gertrude,
for all the women who were buried in their
living bodies, hiding sexual hysteria from doctors
who performed surreptitious clitorectomies,
or sewed their lips over the tiny bud of ecstacy
so men might go on supreme through
thrusting centuries,
for you,
rain of the womb, spindle of Aprhrodite,
bud of Venus, tree of Daphne, moon of Diana,
I chant the song of the three, "Tender Buttons,"
the sign of the trinity:
      "THE NIPPLE, THE NIPPLE, THE CLITORIS,"
and *The Holy Ghost*
is *"The Mother of Us All!"*

OH, ANUS, THROUGH THE CENTURIES

>—for Yang Chu, famed Taoist philospher of the 4th century who, according to Lieh Tzu, said:
>
>*"I wonder if cosmically an idea is any more important than the bowels."*

Oh, anus, through the centuries
men have smuggled diamonds in you
and dope. Homosexuals have written odes
to your sensational glories.

But, I have never wanted more from you
than a comfortable passage
of the wasted fuel of my life
as death the exquisite trap door
opens for the fall through eternity:
exit from life,
light into darkness,
contrast, perception,
crucifixion, resurrection.

The iris of the eye
opens as you—
the flower of the body.

The flower in the eye
opens to let in sight,
and you,
the flower of the body
to let out shit,
and from sight,
from shit,
come flowers
most awesome as they bloom themselves
to death.

THE OLIVE BRANCH

falls from the wet mouth of the old dove
and sinks into a river of fire rushing toward the delta
where the oceans will catch flame and evaporate with lust
and the children's lungs will be sucked of oxygen,
but the president doesn't notice. His polished desk
blinds him with veneer.

And on the street the crowds rush to glimpse the television
screen alight with the fire of electricity
like the body politic
as it broadcasts the baseball scores.

It's the final playoff of the *World Serious*
and we are here, all of us with flesh eyeballs alight
with the wings of the dove as they flutter on beyond
the red and blue sunset
which continues to outdo itself year after year
since the mastodons crept from the sea of blood
baring mammalian breasts full of warm white milk
for all the many colored faces of earth,
children as they suck life from leaves of grass
withering now in the threat of fire or ice,
eternal winter which comes to each, one by one,
but need not be passed in one blast of heat to all the young
buds of being wafting perfumes as they burn
from bright autumn rust, beauty so enough
that it kills the caring heart with its own ceasing.

PART III: WORD WOUNDS AND WATER FLOWERS:

I had a dream, which was not all a dream.
The bright sun was extinguished, and the stars
Did wander darkling in the eternal space,
Rayless, and pathless; and the icy Earth
Swung blind and blackening in the moonless air;
Morn came and went—and came, and brought no day. . . .

Lord Byron from "Darkness"

WORD WOUNDS AND WATER FLOWERS

I.

Where can mad money be spent
on windless meadows, vaporized forests,
under dusty snow falling forever acid,
when love sucked from bleached bones
in ashes floats in particles of lips,
songs, paintings or poems for eons
on and on to nowhere's nothing . . . ?

I can't comprehend nothing of nothing.
"*Non capisco nulla di niente,*"
my Italian grandmother said
before she died at sixty-five
of emphysema from her coal stove
burning through the cold
of dark winters like the eternal one to come
exploding from Godhead to warhead
through centuries of silly soft women
powder-puffed and waiting for men
to come and come, and now they may come
no more . . . to smell perfumed grasses, or see
breasts of velvet blue mountains, red sunsets
or morning's rise after night closes their eyes
forever, Mother Earth, yes, Capitol Earth, I spell you
rich with color, mood and mud.
Slime and beauty beyond mortal words
from which we come with our ears and tongues,
giving ears and tongues to children
and sleek weapons that could demolish us
to metaphorless similes of dust.

II.

Walt Whitman's voice extolled these states and stars
as Democratic Vistas—but they were stolen

from the Redman who reaps cancerous lungs from mined uranium,
and fire water spills from Her green hills,
polluted valleys, fields of waving grain,
full of nitrates, purple mountains majesty, America, plump woman,
your cornucopia fills with poisons, spills
with nuclear barons' oil kills,
distilling carcinogens from landfills full of greed's garbage.
Dolphins, seals, and sea otters breed P.C.B.s. Exxons and G.E.s
P.R. lies and missiles labeled "Peacemakers" that can sizzle
billions in an instant, killing all forever fools of nothing,
no
thing,
unimaginable as zero so profound,
all Promethean longings go unbound.

III.

Have you noticed how angry women are now
between their laughters,
tears loom among their witches' brooms,
because they feel the end approaching all.
It makes their gonads reel with rage.
Since there's too little love for berries, peaches, melons,
mud, and disillusioned children, women have less hope
about the future as their intuition throbs between their legs
forced open to keep life coming from legislated bodies, gates
to heaven or hell, since Satan fell from grace,
into Eden's apple trees and Eve fell on her knees
before him in male mythologies of misogynistic verse.
Earth, so little loved and cursed, She'll explode
with manufactured greed for plastic fruits and flowers, polymers,
poisonous whims of monolithic powers,
money mad with mad money
grabbed by Morgan, Bechtel, whose name
rhymes with hell, Grumman, Hughes,
who helps hold the fuse, AT&T who owns me
and thee, down to our bones.
Executives profits for motifs and motives
to please the very rich with more riches, and mutants,
birth defects of agent orange or irradiating bomb tests—

as astrophysicists describe a black hole
sucking everything to entropy—
and a gap in the ozone layer of climatology
widens as acid rain kills lakes and forests and aflotoxins
like alien enemies, biological warfare agents rain
back down on us. All poisonous greed can't be flushed
away in a Rabelaisian toilet of the universe,
as it comes back to curse our children, poor or rich in one
uni-
verse
all that matters us into matters beyond us
and our separated nations
as each child of us, comes in innocence, dumb with beauty
and the notion of all motion, centrifugal force,
unites nations, flagged by the same photo of Earth
from outer space, mother of an entire race of one
blessed or cursed Earth, Mother of Us, All
oceanic womb-
man to all children
and we are one in all and only all in one is won.

IV.

There's no exotic enemy!
No "them" and "we."
Just ourselves, deep in "us"
a fascination with the exotic other—
dwells in dark sentiment—this passion
with the blood of the other
stains our hands and tongues.
We poke at the fruit, to see
its juices run on the ground,
tear the rose from its stem, scatter petals to the wind,
pluck the butterfly's wings for the microscope's lens,
plunge a fist into a teetering tower of bricks,
watch the debris sail, explode fireworks
until all crumbles to dust and is undone, open
to the curious eye. Does this or that creature die as I die,
cry as I cry, writhe as I would if my guts were ripped
from the walls of my flesh, my ripe heart eaten alive.

The probing questions of sacred exploration,
as if science can *progress*
without *empathy*. Does a penis feel as a clitoris feels?
Do slanted eyes see as I see? Is a white or black skin
or sin the same as a red one; is it like me? Does it burn,
does it peel, does it boil in oil or reel in pain?
The obsession to possess the other so completely
that his blood fills the mouth and you eat of her flesh
from its bone, and then know if she, if he, feels as you feel
if your world is real.

V.

These are the word wounds,
roots of mushroom clouds to rise
from the pockmarked earth:
"*Guinea, dago, spick, nigger, polack, wasp, mick,
chink, jap, frog, kraut, russkie red, bastard, kike,
bitch, macho pig, gimp, fag, dike, cunt, prick,*"
word wounds to make stench of flesh follow
sprayed dust of children's eyes
melted from wondering sockets, animal skin, thighs,
men's hands, women's sighs
roasted in a final feast of fire
beasts caught like lemmings
in a leap to Armageddon's
false resurrection.
Word wounds rise from visions of charred lips,
burnt books, paper ashes, crumbled libraries, stones
under which plastic pens
and computers are fried amid the last cried
words, smoke to pay lip service—
as Orphic light rages
against the dying of the light
and all dust into dust returns
to the last word,
sigh of a burning leaf turning: "Life live,
leaf live, love life leaf live . . ."

VI.

There are those mornings
when the spirit stretches out of itself,
reaches up from the breast, radiates from the groin
beyond sex into song and sensual delight
to see light fall on leaves,
growing green glisten with animal sight
—and the *Romance of Photosynthesis* begins
all beginnings.
There are those afternoons
when knowing beyond saying christens the body
with love for its own breath
and being breathes in harmony with leaves.
There are those evenings when the sunsets with red
and blue glory—even over teeming cities
and glass windows blaze wondrous color,
though children rot in slum gutters
or drug themselves out of the pain
of all that's unfair or insane.

You've smelled the familiar wood, mud, fern aroma,
as red and gold leaves spread a cover over
dried grass and whispering wind on water sings
the stupid and stupendous music of creation,
of an awesome autumn milk-
weed bursts in silk
puffs of seeds and a water spider speeds
patterning the water mirroring your face
amidst scarlet fringes of a maple flecked with green,
serene skies utterly blue with the lies of our lives.
You've seen, heard, felt such awe and you, too,
know wounds of words can burst in fire.
You're tired, too, of trying to speak
the language of leaves as you grow older like me—
lichens blooming on the side of a dead tree.
So, sing a song of peace with me, please,
because death turns to beauty in the dying leaves
and moss is soft and inviting. Tell me, toll me,
please, listen with me to the leaves

aching with eyes and animal sighs
and cries for mercy in the fall from grace
to this quiet, quiet place.

VII.

There are still those days when peace reigns
in desire's mouth and nothing more is longed for
beyond the taste of color, music of hearts and lungs,
sigh of sun, wet of water, touch of the sea, sweet
juice squeezed on the tongue. Then
the body is possessed by light
until the pitcher of sleep fills with milk
poured into the moon and a song of sleep
glows in the throat—giving night its breathy music,
as tortured beasts howl far off in city caverns,
cries from eyes where genitals are plucked flowers
crushed by sadistic curiosity, bled
into troubled sleep. The child
melted by synthetic doom shrieks.
A premeditated alchemic act devised
to sear human flesh, mutates the baby's body
into horror. Brilliantly, germs are bred in laboratories
to foul enemy armies with venereal disease; prostitutes lurk
on the edges of military bases which protect the rich
from the rich—selling flesh like excrement.

VIII.

In civilized rooms,
rich executives wage secret money wars,
deal drugs for profits—devils disguised by designer clothes
live elegant lives that keep the poor unfed
and laboring in heat—fountains of their sweat
fed to gun lords who want more and more
corpses of untimely death buried in pieces under flowering trees
without eyes, hands, guitars or slippers.
Those who die tortured will scream in all our nightmare dreams
until brutes are bred into angels, and prisons emptied of agony,
workers clothed with more than chains, until

puppet dictators lose their strings,
until sparrows sing like nightingales,
and fly like herons above the war for crumbs,
—until I learn to love you with your different body,
your disposition imperfect as mine,
until then, death will go on wearing the soldier's uniform
of his illustrious career—a salute masks his leer.
Like a bullfighter he carves
the mighty bull, to still the beast
with graceful cunning, his sleek
sword hidden in his silk cape.
His missiles poised in their silos
empty of grain, filled with fires of the final feast
he'll eat with his cavernous mouth, carnivorous teeth.
His masculine chin chews children, spits
their wasted bones into cinders, swallows
their budding bodies, and the honey of their
breath as it expires, drips blood as saliva from his lips,
a blistered grin. In his hand, he juggles
the blue and crystal ball full of swirling waters,
over a steel and concrete gravestone
where all our names are inscribed with Dante,
Mozart, Bach, Beethoven, Lady Murasaki,
Emily Dickinson, Rembrandt, Madame Curie,
Einstein, Luther King, Chi'u Chin or Ghandi . . .
fading into dust beyond the last stupendous flash
of life urges into cocky deadly fireworks,
eternal winter, as names
and the word could become in the space of moments,
syllables to no one and nothing perceives
light or darkness, as you and I, love, caress
each others' eyes before we touch, hand on smile inventing love.
But cold and silent of human song the planets could spin
unknown to anyone or anything—
fragile as our flesh which thrills with love's
impulse, electric touch of empathy's
mysterious imagery, waters flowing mind
which cannot dream "nothing" without thinking "zero"
as a perfect some-
thing of the algebraic kind.

IX.

We are all one human creature
bound by one earth
under one sun—moon mutant nations where all children's
ears hear "Songs of Innocence,"
as corporational apes of toxic wastes
breathe alchemic greed bloated powers bigger
than all our tiny flesh made lives,
or little seeds of giant *Sequoia* trees,
most ancient living things of earth,
older than king's tombs, true cathedrals
of the blue Pacific as she rocks, swirling
melodies with the Atlantic's green currents,
currencies . . . rain songs, sounds swell wells,
lakes, faucets, brooks' runes, oceans' tunes,
mystic drafts of summer wetness, cool drink seeping
into thirst,
Earth
nearly all water of which we are made one human
bound by one wet planet
under one maddening moon,
under one arrogant sun,
under one pale watery moon,
under one
bright thirsty sun.

PART IV: THROUGH THE "I" OF THE NEEDLE

"Hold on to dreams
For if dreams die,
Life is a broken
Winged bird
And cannot fly."

Langston Hughes

"The wind? I am the wind. The sea and the moon?
I am the sea and the moon. Tears, pain, love, bird-
flights? I am all of them. I dance what I am.
Sin, prayer, flight, the light that never was on land
or sea? I dance what I am."

from a poem, *Isadora Duncan,* by Carl Sandburg

WHEAT

I hadn't watched maggots
closely before.

The way they squirm and burrow
their way in.

What curious things!

How characteristic of sperm.

Somehow,

how like wheat!

MATRIMONIAL BED

He thinks of her, a furry animal—her center
soft, warm with worry—
but wet, inviting wonder,
a place he can fill with himself.
She feels his need pressed between her thighs,
waiting to be opened by his touch, his fingers will the thrill
of her desire—light explodes
a sunburst in her dark mind—
her face like a winter when she worries
about all the murdered flowers torn flesh tortured shrieks—
her skin like a spring blooming petals, pitying
pink, yellow, purple veined
buds of beneficent being, his red heart burns him
with life she forces like an indigestible summer of merciless heat.

She thinks how mean and hard he seems at times
and pulls herself in and closes
wanting him to open her with his need
and then he rubs her back and neck
and she hears his sweet murmur
as she longs to be strong enough to mother him
and his seed always waiting to spill into her
and make her bloom like a round melon of light
that talks and sees roses which must die to be
beautiful like the sea from which she smells
her own body throbbing and rolling
as he thrusts need into her need to be kneaded
necessary as bread to earth planted in spring so that grass
grows for the eating of all things vibrant in the green sun
of summer festering with insects, birds, blossoms, sticky throated
buds oozing sap from her lap full of flowers, syllables spill
prattled from small round tongues, animals that come
seeing out of her breathing belly—laughing, weeping, seeping songs
and dances of pleasure, pain wonder—bleeding in and out
of the mystery that only skies can know,
only mountains touch,
only stars breathe.

YOUR BODY

has a strength
destined to know me.
Wherever my lips touch you
they find a kiss
as if my hands
had made you of clay
exactly
as I would have wished.

Your hands, your arms,
your chest, thighs,
your special parts
are missing parts of me,
vessel into which you fit,
one river of two streams
flowing into one ocean.

Before we met,
I was on the verge
of automation.
As metal I'd have rusted,
atrophied.

As flesh,
I'll stay alive unto death
feeling your hands kneading me
to breath.

THE FISHBLOOD OF A WOMAN

The blood of a fish is like
the blood of a bleeding woman.
But we call fish cold blooded
and a mother's love has the
hottest blood in the galaxy.

The seagull's squeal is like
the squeal of a newborn child—
tormented,

and the blood of a man
is like the blood of a wandering gull
hunting free and hunted.

All blood is red so that we can see it,
and anger is red
so that we can know it
and all bleeding blood is angry
like the wound of war.

PREGNANCY AND OLD MEN

They want to have the babies when they are old,
though the cocks of the walk,
their breasts and bellies grow, good Papas,
into womanhood, emotions are let go
like tears that run down steel swords gone dull.

Their eyes brighten with pretty daughters
who sparkle like their mates did long ago.
They want to be pregnant with girlish life,
to feel themselves rise quick again
just at the thought. These men women
have expected to be perfect for them,
creatures of confused mother love,
searching for the breast of Honeysuckle summer
again, longing which grows into
fleeting gold, then silver snow.

I keep having a dream of an old woman, anxious rhapsody,
disapproving of me, and wake
to realize I have grown old
enough to disapprove of my younger self
full of mistakes, and the dust
is flying, radio-active everywhere. I can't
shovel the snow fast enough to get back on the road.
I left the windows open and the car's buried
inside and out with snow, snow, snow
and dark comes soon. Everyone I ask gives
a different direction on the roads. Cold.
I can't remember any of the ways.
I'm too old for babies now.

Sun on leaves is enough for me
if profits before children and trees
don't waste all to nothing, I'll listen
to Vivaldi concertos to fill

my aging years. I'll make Japanese water colors,
or sing along with birds, learn their tunes and colors:
iridescent Magpie, Black-capped Chickadee
chirping in a narrow pine tree, Great Blue Heron or Jay,
Red-tailed Hawk, Screech Owl, Mourning Dove,
Ruby-Throated Hummingbird, Indigo Bunting,
Scarlet Tanager, Redbellied Woodpecker, Yellow-bellied
Sapsucker, White-breasted Nuthatch, Redwinged Blackbird,
Brown Creeper, Golden-crowned Kinglet,
each with his own personality
like the tiny pink mouse, in my daughter's snake cage
waiting to be eaten for a desert snake's prey.
We are all like that, struggling on our backs waiting
to be blown by greed to dust or snow
as we grow old and some say there's *nothing*
beyond flesh gone dry.

There *are* leaf patterns,
bubbles baked into the bread,
chemical variegations
even as the mouse is slowly ingested,
mammalian blood becomes reptilian,
all churns in cauldrons of smoke and dreams.

How intricately a snake loops,
what a slow moving toward death,
what cannibal embrace,
the mouse's head in the snake's,
what a quick moving toward death,
what a slow moving
toward life,
what a quick ending is death.
Please
let the children live.
Everyone
who's sane
loves
them.

APERTURE

—for Annie and Jim Wright

I attempt to rearrange the past in Venetian Palaces
built by blood thirsts or delicate lusts,
full of plaintive strains of Monteverdi
trilled in Gothic arches.
Through a camera's eye
I look backward on hope,
every lost stroke between us
mesmerizes mind
into something fair and kind—
as here, in the present, dying drones
drone in autumn sun,
leaves rot, purple asters turn to grey seed—
like tiny mushroom clouds dotting umber and sienna land-
      scapes of late autumn, muddled earth
      with the garbage of greed
everywhere, crushed cans, chemical poisons, wasted paper,
but in my mind, dusk pours in slanted light of high windows,
twilight motes dance amid red velvet curtains
in Venetian Palaces above shimmering waters, narrow streets,
we lie embracing, intertwined forever
until darkness erases us,
the woods here in dark.
The stamina of memory opens an aperture,
a window on forever, before
the nuclear age
when only a burnt out
floating of Earth toward Vega,
after the sun was done,
was an end so far off
it couldn't be
imagined.

WAKE ME UP IN A HUNDRED YEARS

when I've grown a green
kelp sea-green beard.
Just let me lie here by the sea
in sand beneath
a constant acclimation of wing to wind
currents carrying gulls cries
as a Cormorant cuts across sky
oh, wake me up
in a hundred
years
when
I've
grown a green
kelp sea-green beard
among the dunes
of time and sun
among the dunes of seaswept runes
among the dunes of seas and times
among eternal windswept ryhmes
among forever singing chimes
after all the human crimes
are done.

A WOMAN'S BUTTOCKS

—for Virginia Woolf

I have some wild notion of following the birds
to the rim of the world,
flinging myself on the spongy turf there
and drinking forgetfulness
until roots twine around my knees
and worm their way deep inside me.
My mind spills like hot coffee over the saucer
of my life and drowns in its own dark ecstacy.

Lulling my pain with the aspirin of death
taken in small doses nightly,
I sit beside the fire of your soul,
glowing flesh in the light,
never quite awake.

A match struck behind my eyelids
flares against my retinas.
A shadow dance of puppets begins:
mother, father, child, lover
whirl in a Chinese lantern show
until the frenzy that would burn me quickly
in a puff of ecstasy reels away.

Spun out in a slow red river of sound
from the mouth of longing, I used to measure my time
in monthly cycles, forging a link, a secret transaction
of modems, voice answering screen. I talk to you as if to
myself, stammering an answer. I try laboriously to bear
wheat, voice to breath, tongue to tongue.

We end as a feather floats from the sky,
vaults the dark pool of mind, reflecting the moon
like a woman's buttocks turned up again to heaven.

THE TREES ARE DYING

Yes. It's true. Sugar maples are disappearing. Too
many chemicals! "The trees, trees, trees"
are all I want to look at and know, says Jerzey Spacive,
Hungarian linguist dying of AIDS
after surviving Nazi Germany's
camps for Jews. "I can't even listen to music!"
says he. "I anticipate all the notes
that fade into nothing. No thrill
comes from classic sound that used to comfort me.

Just the sunlight, moonlight, sunset on the trees,
they're all I want to know, all I see. The trees
are everything to me. The last sight for all should be of trees,
Bartlett pear trees, pyrus with their sweet golden fruit
dropping from thick glossy greenery, pointed leaves
with fringes folded inward like arms on my breast."

"Yes, apple trees in the orchard on
the horizon. Hazelnut, Hickory,
Poplar, Rock Oak, Blue Spruce, Blue Juniper,
Red Cedar, Yewberry, Ashberry,
Red Oak and White Oak, Red Pine and Grey Pine,
White and Black Birch,
aromatic Eastern Hemlocks dying of a blight,
Rare Elms and Douglas Firs, Redwoods
cut for timber, phenomenal ancient
Sequoia Gigantia felled for silly furniture.
Rain forests murdered for grazing meat."

*"A twenty-five percent decline and a loss
of nearly half of new trees
over the past thirty years," the forester told me.
"Synthetic chemicals begin to appear
in their rings at the dawn*

of the Industrial Revolution—poisons
traced to the Ohio River Valley, airborne
to the Northeastern forests . . . ."

Jerzey murmurs as he slips into his forever sleep:
"Seeds of the endangered Whitebark Pine of the high Rockies
are a staple of the grizzly bears, red squirrels,
and song birds, here, and there.
The dark green aromatic Hemlocks are falling to an Asian blight,
wooly adelgid and fiorinia scale, which also invites
infestation by spider mites,
and so the Eastern Hemlocks go
the way of the American Elm from its Dutch Disease,
and the Chestnuts before them perished, too.
The trees are going to entropy, acid rain, chemicals and PCBs.

The trees are all that comfort me.
They hold all the answers unspoken in their branches.
Trees make time visible and fragrant, they are our breath
and breathe with us as we breathe they live
and we live as they breathe and greed is killing them.
The trees hold all the answers.
Ask them. We enter the grove and are changed,
peace rains down in green over us. Green which holds the mountains
together with roots, green which scatters lacy shade over us, spins
out our breath in freshened sips.
We drink the rain with them.
Beware, the trees are dying with us.
Every sapling rises up to breathe with every child in
its rightful place under the sun,
set me free
into the arms of my Copper Beech tree."

ANSWER TO THE SUICIDE

"I will nothing to no one."
—Jorge Luis Borges

In the morning
there will be sunlight.
There will be day.
One evening
I'll die
and the sum total of the universe
will continue.

I'll erase my ears, eyes, nose,
tongue, fingers,
but the continents, mountains, music,
pyramids will persist.

Behind me
the future will accumulate.
In earth like a man in a woman,
I'll make food
out of food.

When I see the last sunrise,
I'll hear the first bird.
I will everything
to everyone.

SHANGRI-LA

As we begin our trip
to Shangri-la, then hope
that the way is long
down mountain streams where the water
is fresh with adventure,
up pathways to where wisdom gathers
on mountaintops. Let's not fear
the nightmares
sent by xenophobic monsters
invented by projected greed.
We will not meet them on our path
if our spirits are aloof
and sensual emotions touch
our bodies
with each other's hopes.
Come, swim with me in the cool lake as we age with youth
and then let's watch the sunsets, red-orange and blue,
purple as dawn, in our own magical garden
which borders the gardens of others,
where we work renewed, never judging the monsters
we meet in our nightmares.

Perhaps we'll never greet the Lochness Monster
or Big Foot, Tyrannosaurus Rex,
Dracula or black-booted Nazi,
bigoted Skinhead or exorcising priest
of exclusive nonsense and *gobbledegook*,
fierce fascist, or self-righteous fanatic,
if we refuse them transport,
if our spirits stay vigilant, watching over
our body's good work, touch others
with joy here and now, and forgive and live
close to the Earth and all her gifts,
sunsets and rises, apples,
pears, corn, wheat, rice,
things that matter to children.

THE LILY SHIVERS

on the autumn pond afloat with shrivelled leaves.
Nothing stays.

Feelings in the blood drain
from the corpse as seeds fall
beneath dead leaves.
Love is half of longing.

When we are together,
longing goes
as a sunset sinks behind a mountain top
leaving a halo glow.
Seeds root beneath rotting leaves.

I must be careful
not to long for the ache
of wanting you, to lick the sweetness
which is gone from me, to miss
the wish
which is unfulfilled
more than savor its repose,
here, now,
the sun on the autumn pond,
an iridescent duck with his mallard brown
mate amidst the dying leaves,
lilies still bright with beauty shiver as they go
into winter,
thrilling with the cold that will
come when it will come,
as necessary as the setting of the sun.

WOMAN FROM MY WOMB

daughter child full grown
of my very flesh
into your own
separate being,
seeing
me as free
from your need of me.

Now, I need you
to feel,
my mother's need of you,
as I return to the dark
of my lonely widow's room
to day dream of your visits
offering spring flowers
to my granite tomb.

DANCING SONG FOR MY DAUGHTER

—After Gabriela Mistral

Stars dance their light
The night sky shivers.
Listening to waves,
dance, my daughter!

Wind wanders fields
singing in the wheat.
Hearing the winds song,
dance, my daughter.

Earth spinning holds
children in her skirts.
Feeling the moon's hands,
dance, my daughter.

Love winning fills
all with Her power.
Seeing Her sunrise,
dance, my daughter.

Love losing sighs
in wet wounded eyes.
Burying my bones, smile
and dance, my daughter.

SHAMAN'S SONG

> *"The dancer of the future will dance*
> *the freedom of women . . . I see America dancing."*
> —Isadora Duncan

I danced with ears in my belly,
sang songs from a sonorous throat.
Academicians thought I was crazy.
Men imagined I was being sexy.
They sent me foolish invitations
which lead no where.
I tore them up laughing.

As Mirabei, at the shrine of my navel,
I worshipped the leaves that flowed through me.
I lived as the symbiotic tree.
I've dedicated my body and soul
to the American Demeter.
I sent Her radiance through rythmic muscles
out into the universe.
I worshipped Her redwood forests, Her
Natural Cathedrals, the fruit of Her fields,
the labors of Her women,
Her Indians and immigrants.

My Goddess was the good Earth.
I came from Her milk, Her breasts.
Hypatia gave me the spirit to dance
with my soul in my belly.
I smelled Earth's music, heard Her colors,
tasted Her fire and knew
the dancer *is* the dance.

AS WHEN SOME SILENCED SINGER HEARS HER ARIA

—for *Vittoria Colonna
Naples/Ischia, 1492-1547

or creatures crawl riding foam to hurry back to salty home,
as oceans pound fruit to pecking pipers,
or shells keep tunes in earlike chambers,
filled with sand and sea to roam
like songs rejoicing feathered nest and comb
as warm eggs crack chirping hunger, and a child slithers
forth to touch, smell, see, hear earthly cries and laughters
pushed suckling free from nurturing womb—

my tongue is loosed beyond a private caroling, my pen prances
urged by mysterious love as if it had no part in what is sighed
as Earth sings praises through me, my eyes are green sea,
red skies, wildflowers, a child who dances
well when loved beyond the pain of men's tribal wars, pride,
threatened suicide, and bloody rivalry.

Vittoria Colonna is emulated in the Petrachan style of sonnet. Daughter of the Grand Constable of Naples, and born in Rome, she was married to the Marquis of Pescara, and had two happy youthful years, on the island of Ischia, with her husband before constant invasions by Spain, France, and Germany, resulted in his imprisonment and involvement in wars of resistance. She carried on a long correspondence in prose and verse with her absent husband who was wounded and died in battle in 1525. She retired to Ischia where her grief and love for her husband found expression in her sonnets. She never remarried, but had many admirers, among them Michelangelo, who dedicated some of his finest sonnets to her. Her collection of poems, which appeared in 1538, was the first volume of poetry by a European woman to be published and widely read.

THROUGH THE "I" OF THE NEEDLE

The peach is
a belly dancer's fruit.
It has a navel eye for seeing
the world through the skin,
rounded buttocks
good
to place against the hand
the way earth reminds flesh
of its being.

Through the eye of the needle,
death is a country
where people
wonder
and worry
what it's like to live.

The sullen wish to live
and live soon
to be done
with death
and the happy
want
to stay dead
forever
wondering
will it hurt
to live
and is there death
after
death?

ABOUT THE AUTHOR

DANIELA GIOSEFFI, poet, novelist, editor, critic, multimedia performer, educator—achieved critical acclaim for her first book of poems, *Eggs in the Lake* (Boa Editions, Ltd., Brockport, NY, 1979). Nona Balakian, for whom the National Book Critic's Circle Award in criticism has been named—former reviewer for *The New York Times* and author of *Critical Encounters*—wrote of Gioseffi's first book of poetry: *"One of the finest new poets around. Her work overflows with poetic vision. Nothing is ever pretentious or done for effect. She's achieved what the surrealists hoped for poetry."* Gioseffi's novel, *The Great American Belly*, was published by Doubleday & Dell, New York, New English Library, London, and Graficki zavod Hrvastske, Zagreb, 1977-79. Larry McMurtry, Pulitzer and National Book Award Winner, called the novel: *"Engaging, filled with energy . . . irresistable writing,"* in *The Washington Post*.

Gioseffi was a featured speaker on world peace and disarmament at the Barcelona International Bookfair, 1990, and the Miami International Bookfair, 1991, where she was presented with an *American Book Award* for her edited and annotated, international compendium *Women on War* (Touchstone, Simon & Schuster, New York, London, 1988, and Weiner Frauenverlag, Vienna, 1992). Carl Sagan called it: *"A book of searing analyses and cries from the heart. . . ."* She has presented her work from the University of Venice to the BBC at Oxford and been interviewed by *El Pais,* Madrid. She began her career as a journalist in Selma, Alabama, 1961, during the civil rights movement, integrating Southern television. She's worked in the Gandhian world peace and justice movement ever since.

Her book, *On Prejudice: A Global Perspective* (Anchor Doubleday, New York, London and Japan 1993) won a grant award from The Ploughshares Fund: World Peace Foundation. Her translations of the Caribbean poet, Carilda Oliver Labra, *Dust Disappears*, with a foreword by Gregory Rabassa, will appear from Cross-Cultural Communications, Merrick, New York, in 1995. Her poems have been published in magazines and anthologies throughout the US and Europe. Her poetic plays, "The Sea Hag in the Cave of Sleep" and "Daffodil Dollars" have been produced Off-Broadway. She lived for nearly thirty years in New York City before settling back in her home state of New Jersey. Through the 1980s, Gioseffi served on the nominating committee for *The Olive Branch Book Awards* of the Writers and Publishers Alliance. She has been a professional actress, dancer, singer composing lyrics for the poet's harp. She's been heard on National Public Radio; CBC Canada; and the BBC (UK). She won PEN's 1990 Short Fiction Award for "Daffodil Dollars" (from her stories: *The Psychic Touch*), aired on N.P.R.'s "The Sound of Words." Her poems, stories, criticism, essays, and interviews have appeared in major press books from Houghton Mifflin, Viking, William Morrow, Harper & Row, Oxford University Press, Faber & Faber, Doubleday, Simon & Schuster, and in leading periodicals, such as *The Paris Review, Ms., The Nation, Confrontation, Contact II, Antaeus, Choice, American Book Review, VIA, The New York Times*, and *Library Journal* for twenty-seven years.